HERALD BIBLICAL BOOKLETS

Robert J. Karris O.F.M., General Editor

THE

APOCALYPSE

by

ELISABETH SCHUESSLER FIORENZA

FRANCISCAN HERALD PRESS

1434 West 51st St. • Chicago, Ill. 60609

The Apocalypse, by Elisabeth Schuessler Fiorenza.
Copyright © 1976 by Franciscan Herald Press,
1434 West 51st Street, Chicago, Illinois 60609.

Made in the United States of America.

Library of Congress Cataloging in Publication
Data:

Fiorenza, Elisabeth Schuessler, 1938-
  The apocalypse.

  (Herald Biblical booklets)
    1. Bible. N. T. Revelation—Criticism,
interpretation, etc. I. Title.
BS2825.2.F5   1976   228'.06   76-16802
ISBN 0-8199-0726-X

NIHIL OBSTAT:
  Mark Hegener O.F.M.
  Censor

IMPRIMATUR:
  Msgr. Richard A. Rosemeyer, J.D.
  Vicar General, Archdiocese of Chicago

June 18, 1976

TABLE OF CONTENTS

EDITOR'S FOREWORD

For countless Christians the Apocalypse is forbidding and puzzling. It's like quicksand, something to be avoided at all cost. No matter how often they have attempted to read it, it baffles them.

For many other Christians the Apocalypse is the most important book in the Bible. Amidst the manifold uncertainties of our contemporary future-shock society they find security in the message of the Apocalypse. For the Apocalypse, interpreted according to their lights, reveals who the Anti-Christ is, when the world is going to end, and who will be saved.

In this booklet Professor Elisabeth Schuessler Fiorenza shows through clear and incisive analyses of the structure and theology of the Apocalypse that it need not be a forbidding and puzzling book. She is a most competent guide into the forbidding territory of the Apocalypse. Under her astute direction puzzling passage after passage becomes clear and understandable.

As Professor Fiorenza guides her readers through the Apocalypse, they come to see with greater clarity the richness and importance of its theology. The Apocalypse is important for Christians, not because it gives them a time-table and heavenly membership list for the end of the world, but because it challenges them to take the earthly and human dimensions of salvation with utmost seriousness.

THE AUTHOR, Associate Professor of Theology at the University of Notre Dame, has a doctorate in New Testament Studies from the University of Münster. She is a highly regarded authority on the Apocalypse. Her competence in New Testament Studies has been recognized by appointments to the editorial boards of the *Catholic Biblical Quarterly* and the *Journal of Biblical Literature*.

ROBERT J. KARRIS O.F.M.
Catholic Theological Union at Chicago

N.B. Unless otherwise noted, all Scripture quotations are based on the Revised Standard Version.

Chapter I
VARIOUS INTERPRETATIONS OF THE APOCALYPSE

For many Christians the Apocalypse (Apoc) is not only the last book in the New Testament but also the least. Today many readers experience great difficulty in understanding the book. They can apparently make very little theological sense out of the book, and they often fail to gain much spiritual benefit from reading it. The text is indeed difficult to understand. It contains repetitions, doublets, and artificial constructions. The logical flow of thought appears to be interrupted, and the temporal sequence of its visions appears to be disturbed. It not only seems to lack a clear sense of time and development, but its images and symbols also strike one as strange and bizarre.

This difficulty in interpretation is not just experienced in modern times. Shortly after it was written, the Apoc appeared as a highly controversial book with obscure and confused contents. The reader's plight in antiquity has been well summed up' by Jerome, a church father and exegete. In a letter to Paulinus, a bishop of Nola, Jerome writes: "The Apocalypse of John has as many secrets as words" (Ep. LIII, 9). This judgment is as true today as it was then. Its obscure language and its cryptic symbolism have made the Apoc a book "with seven seals" and an esoteric and clandestine revelation. It remains for many ordinary Christians and trained theologians alike a difficult book. It is often conveniently overlooked in preaching and in teaching. It often plays no role in spiritual direction and meditation. At best it is seen as a curiosity that accidentally and embarrassingly belongs to the New Testament (NT).

a. Popular understandings of the Apoc

Many have not only labelled the book as unintelligible or crude but have also considered it subchristian or not even Christian, since the author speaks of divine wrath and fierce revenge but not of God's love and grace. They agree with Martin Luther wro wrote in 1522: "My spirit cannot accommodate itself to this book. There is one sufficient reason for the small esteem in which I hold it — that Christ is neither taught in it nor recognized." This verdict is echoed in contemporary NT scholarship which has widely neglected the book and has rarely used it to understand the history of early Christianity and its beliefs.

Nevertheless, the Apoc has not been merely the object of misunderstanding, neglect and rejection. It has been greatly appreciated by artists and sectarians alike. It is the one book in the NT which has inspired great works of literature, music, and art. Its rhythmic and archaic language, its repetitions of sound and words, and its wealth of colors, symbols and image-associations have brought it to the attention of artists throughout the centuries and have given it a place in the

8

anthology of world literature. This poetic and dramatic character of the book can be best perceived when the text is read aloud as the author intended it to be. Its surrealistic symbols and strange images may be difficult to be reproduced by the pictorial painter but can be appreciated by the modern artist. Its visions of the "new land" and "New Jerusalem" have found resonance in the music and poetry of oppressed and suffering people.

Whereas established Christianity often remains helpless in the face of its message, the Apoc is read again and again by sectarian fringe groups and marginal Christians. The book plays a great role in Christian fundamentalist groups and in revolutionary Christian circles. The fundamentalists find in the Apoc exact predictions of the end of the world and of the events which must precede the end. They often use or misuse the book as a time-schedule for the last days to which they alone have the right key. Moreover, since they claim to possess the right understanding of the book, they do not hesitate to concretely identify, for example, the beast of the Apoc with communism or with our immoral society and to associate the elect of the New Jerusalem with their own righteous group or with America and its ideals. A few years ago I received an invitation to participate in a TV show on the Apoc. When I inquired why they planned to do such a show, I was informed that in Texas a cloud formation had appeared which had the form of a cross. A sure sign of the impending end and judgment!

9

When I argued with the person who invited me that the Apoc does not expect the sign of the cross to appear in heaven before the last day, I lost my one chance of appearing on a TV show on the Apoc. The place of the final eschatological revelation had to be Texas.

Yet the Apoc has not only influenced the patriotic fundamentalists on the right, but it has impressed even more those sectarians on the left who are critical of their own society and church, because they project evil not on outside enemies but seek it in their own midst. These millenial movements experience their world and society as dominated by evil, by tyrannous powers of demonic dimensions with boundless destructiveness. The sufferings of the victims will become more and more untolerable until suddenly the hour will come when under the leadership of a prophet the oppressed will rise up, overthrow the tyrannic powers, and inherit dominion over the earth. A millenial movement always claims at least partially to embody in itself the eschatological reign of God. Thus both the rightist as well as the leftist sectarian groups claim now the dominion over the earth which the Apoc promises for the eschatological future. But whereas for the rightist the kingdom belongs to established society, for those on the left it belongs to the underdogs who are exploited and oppressed by this society.

A final popular way to read and to understand the Apoc is to spiritualize, internalize, and to individualize the images, promises and threats of the book. We are all probably familiar with the illustration of Apoc 3:20, where Jesus is seen standing before the door of the soul and asking to be admitted, even though the text refers not to spiritual communion but promises eschatological table community. Similarly the soul is often likened to the "bride of the Lamb" or the New Jerusalem, images and symbols which refer in the Apoc to eschatological salvation. Any careful study of the Apoc shows that the tenor of the book is not individualistic or spiritualistic, but cosmic and worldwide. The visions of the Apoc cannot be reduced to anthropology.

b. Scholarly interpretations of the Apoc

Exegetes have generally shared the perplexities and pitfalls encountered by the ordinary reader. For a long time theologians assumed that the Apoc describes the events of church history or world history until the last day. Others maintained that the book is a theological work and presents us with the main data and events of salvation history or gives us the principles of a philosophy of history. Most exegetes today assume that the book is oriented toward the final eschatological events which the author expected in his own lifetime. The Apoc addresses the situation of readers contemporary with the author and promises them the speedy return of their Lord. By pointing to the nearness of the final eschatological salvation, the author seeks to encourage his fellow Christians who are threatened with imminent persecution.

No generally recognized and accepted agreement has been reached with respect to the composition and the blue-print which the author had in mind in writing the book. The same perplexity remains not only with respect to certain images or passages of the book, but also with regard to its total theological perspective. The variety of proposals and interpretations that continue to be offered by scholars substantiates the judgment that despite many serious studies few primitive Christian writings have remained so elusive.

There exists, however, agreement that the Apoc has to be studied from a literary and historical point of view. The assumption that the author wrote the whole book down either during or after his visions as it was dictated to him, is discarded today in exegetical circles. The Apoc is clearly a literary composition and theological work of an author who gleaned his materials from the Old Testament, from Jewish Apocalypticism, from pagan mythological sources, and from early Christian faith and praxis.

Source and tradition critical analyses maintain that the Apoc is composed of small written or oral units. They attempt to solve the logical difficulties and the obscurity of the composition with its repetitions and cross-references by postulating different sources, different redactional processes, or different traditional schemata which one or more redactors put together more or less skillfully. Other scholars reject this patchwork-hypothesis and maintain the literary unity of the book by analyzing its style and language and by showing its careful composition and dramatic-symbolic impact on the reader. Whereas source critical, analyses often see the Apoc as a Jewish writing to which minor Christian corrections and details have been added, recent studies of the Christology of the book have demonstrated its genuine Christian outlook and traditions.

Thus the reader who earnestly wishes to study the book is confronted with a bewildering array of scholarly opinion. Yet this absence of agreement does not spell total futility. We always have to keep in mind that the dramatic and symbolic character of the book necessarily defies exact analysis and fixed definitions. The author did not write a tractate or dogmatic work on the "Last Things" but intended to stun us with the power of his images and visions. The symbols and images of the book have evocative character. They not only demand an intellectual response, but they also elicit an emotional and practical response from us as well. The Apoc bodies forth a great vision of the future toward which the churches of Asia Minor and the readers of all times are living. The author did not develop this theological vision in abstract sentences, but expressed it in the language of symbol and myth.

If we are patient enough to study the Apoc on its own terms, we might be able to participate in the vision of the author. In viewing a painting, we have to stand back to grasp the full impact of its colors, forms and relationships, and to comprehend it as a total work of art. Yet after we have viewed the painting in perspective, we have to analyze the details of its composition, figures, and colors and to study the techniques employed by the artist. Such an analysis demands a "close-up" view of the painting which will deepen and enhance our total comprehension of the painting. The same holds true for studying the Apoc. Whereas only the patient hearing and reading of the book as a whole can transmit a total comprehension of its vision and perspective, a careful "close-up" analysis might enhance our understanding and interpretation of the book. The following analysis of the Apoc intends to do just this, namely, to deepen and broaden the emotive and intellectual responses provoked by the symbols and images of the book.

CHAPTER II
THE LITERARY MODEL OR FORM OF THE APOCALYPSE

The form and content of a literary work are intimately bound together. Artists and writers express their experiences and truths in different literary forms: in poems and dramas, in novels and stories, or in slogans and advertisements. The quality of a literary work depends on the interrelationship of content and form. In order to understand a work we have to carefully observe how the author expressed and formulated it. The same is true for the understanding of the Apoc. Any interpretation of the book has to answer the question: What was the literary model or form which the author of the Apoc chose to express his message? In searching for an answer, scholars have suggested that the author had as his model a pastoral letter, a liturgy, the ancient drama, an apocalyptic work, or a prophetic book.

a. The Apoc — A Pastoral Letter

At first glance it appears that the author intended to write an open pastoral letter to seven communities in Asia Minor. This intention is clearly expressed in the beginning of the Apoc. The marks of the ancient letter form are found in the framework of the book. Apoc 1:1-3 serve as title for the whole work. Apoc 1:4-6 form the introduction of the letter in a fully developed and stylized way and are similar to the address of the ancient letter. Such an epistolary introduction is typical of the Pauline literature and was thus already accepted in early Christianity as the proper epistolary form. The address proper first mentions the name of the sender and of the recipients ("John to the seven churches that are in Asia"); then it continues with an opening blessing ("Grace to you and peace from him . . ."); and finally it concludes with a doxology ("To him who loves us and has freed us . . . to him be glory and dominion for ever and ever"). As the author introduced the book with an address and blessing, so he concludes it with final admonitions, warnings, blessings and greetings ("The

15

grace of the Lord Jesus be with all the saints. Amen"). Such a conclusion is likewise similar to that of the Pauline letters. The author, therefore, apparently gave his work the form of a circular letter which he seems to have patterned according to the then already authoritative Pauline letter form.

Nevertheless, the Apoc does not at all read like a circular, pastoral letter. Some exegetes consequently suggest that the epistolary form was added by a final editor only after the work had already been finished. It is only an artificial framework, and the author had a completely different literary model in mind when writing the book.

b. The Apoc — A Liturgy

Since the Apoc is full of cultic symbols and liturgical actions, of hymnic language and doxological formulas, it has been assumed by some that the final literary form of the Apoc reflects a liturgical formulary. They propose for instance that the author chose the early Christian paschal liturgy as the blue-print according to which he structured his book. Others postulate that the outline of the Apoc reflects the Jerusalem temple liturgy or follows the Jewish calendar of feasts. Some scholars consider the Christian worship constitutive for the structure of the book. They suggest that the author used a eucharistic liturgy or a Christian initiation ritual as the basis for his composition. However, most concede that the liturgical pattern represents only one of the structural components of the book and that it was

16

complemented by other patterns and forms.

The author, moreover, never invites the Christians to participate in the heavenly liturgy and the heavenly victory hymns. In the present only a small door in heaven is open through which the seer and his readers can gain a glimpse of the heavenly world. But they have no direct access to that world. Their prayers are mediated through heavenly beings, and the divine interpretations and commands are communicated through angelic mediators. It is true that the Apoc is to be read in a liturgical setting. This setting, however, is the worship of the Christian community which learns by hearing the book of prophecy not to forget their own history and time, but to give them meaning and hope.

c. The Apoc — A Drama

The suggestion that the Apoc is written in the form of the ancient drama is closely related to the liturgical interpretation since in Greek tragedy the roots of drama and cult are intertwined. Interpreters, therefore, have not merely acknowledged the dramatic character of the Apoc, but have maintained that the Apoc is patterned after the Greek drama since it has dramatis personae, stage props, a plot, and a tragic-comic ending. Some consider the Apoc to be a drama of five acts and three scenes, whereas others maintain that seven acts with seven scenes constitute the book. Others propose that the outline of the Apoc and its plot are patterned after the stages and scenes of the imperial games which were celebrated in Ephesus. The most compelling argument for the influence of Greek dramatic forms on the composition of the Apoc is the employment of choruses by the author. Recent studies of the hymnic materials in the Apoc have convincingly demonstrated that the hymns comment and complement the visions and auditions of the book. They function thus in the same way as the choruses in the Greek drama preparing and commenting upon the dramatic movements of the plot.

However, even though the Apoc contains dramatic elements, it is evident that it is not written in the dialogue-form of the drama just as it is not patterned after a certain liturgical formulary. Liturgical and dramatic elements are important for the composition of the Apoc, but they do not constitute it.

d. The Apoc — An Apocalypse

Since the Apoc gave the whole array of apocalyptic literature its name, most scholars maintain that the book belongs to this literary category. Apocalyptic literature was in vogue during the last two centuries before and the first two after Christ. Apocalyptic passages appear in later prophetic works, but the first extensive work known to us is the Book of Daniel. Other examples of this literature are the Book of Henoch, the Secrets of Henoch, the Apocalypse of Baruch or the Fourth Book of Esdras. Apocalyptic thought and hope came to be a major influence not only in Judaism but also in Early Christianity.

This literature was inspired by the expectation of the overthrow of all oppressive, earthly conditions through cosmic catastrophes; it expected the resurrection of the dead and the appearance of a new paradaisal time of salvation. This expectation and hope were expressed, however, in various literary forms and genres. We can trace literary elements which are found in most of the apocalyptic writings, but we can not speak of apocalyptic literature as a definite literary form. The symbolism and mythical images, the codified language and symbolic numbers, the form of vision and audition, the cosmological stage setting and the eschatological expectation and hope for the future doubtlessly characterize the Apoc as an apocalyptic book. Nevertheless, essential elements of apocalyptic literature such as pseudonymity, secrecy, historical periodization, journeys through the heavenly world or lists of revealed things are conspicuously absent in the Apoc.

Of decisive importance is that the author mentions his name, John, four times (1:1,4,9; 22:8). Since he adds no additional honorary titles we can safely assume that the name John designates a personality well known to the readers of the book. Even though the tradition identifies the author with John the Apostle, the author does not identify himself as one of the twelve apostles, and Apoc 21:14 makes such an identification impossible. That the author writes in his own name and authority distinguishes the Apoc from other apocalyptic writings. Apocalyptic authors wrote under a pseudonym and claimed the name of a

19

great figure of the past for their work (e.g., Moses, Elijah, Henoch, Baruch) in order to gain a fictitious standpoint in the past from where they could present surveys of world history in the form of pronouncements for the future. This is not the case with the Apoc. The author clearly characterizes himself as a contemporary of his readers and hearers, to whom the work is addressed (1:9). He is concerned with the present and the immediate future. The only significant event of the past to which he alludes is the death and resurrection of Jesus Christ.

Another distinguishing feature is the fact that the Apoc, unlike other apocalyptic writings, is not a secret book intended only for a few elect and illumined. The book is explicitly addressed to all the communities and designed for public liturgical reading. The author makes a point that the book is "unsealed." In Apoc 22:10 the "sealing" of the book is strictly opposed. The Apoc does not communicate esoteric knowledge, but contains an open exhortation and a clear eschatological message which is related to the concrete situation of the Christians in Asia Minor and their immediate future. The so-called seven letters to the communities, therefore, replace in the Apoc the overviews of world history and the reviews of the heavenly secrets found in other apocalyptic writings.

e. The Apoc — A Christian Prophetic-Apocalyptic Circular Letter

Exegetes are still divided on the question whether or not the author intended his work to be a prophecy or an apocalypse. The author of the Apoc doubtlessly understands himself as a Christian prophet and intends his work to be a "word of prophecy." Moreover, most of the classic prophetic forms are found in the Apoc. It contains prophetic vision reports and messenger speeches, prophetic oracles and symbolic actions, announcements of judgment and proclamations of salvation concerning the present situation of the Christians and the immediate future. We find here prophetic summons, warnings, threats and admonitions, technical legal language as well as hymns of praise, woe oracles, and laments. Exegetical analyses highlight that the author not only uses prophetic language but also patterns whole sections after the prophetic visions of Isaiah, Ezekiel, Zechariah or Daniel.

Like the Hebrew prophets John takes his standpoint in his own day and age. His "word of prophecy" is completely committed to the strengthening of the congregations in Asia Minor in their severe clash with the anti-divine powers actualized in the Roman state and religion. The author thus follows in his book the Early Christian practice of combining admonition with proclamation.

It, therefore, appears to be no accident that the Apoc as a whole has the form of the Pauline letters and that the apocalyptic visions, auditions, symbols and imagery are set in an epistolary framework. The author derives the authority of his work not through employing pseudonymity and fictional time-tables, but by patterning it

21

after the authoritative Pauline letter form. Like the letters of Paul, the Apoc is directed toward concrete problems within the early Christian communities of Asia Minor. Just as the letters of Paul situate the problems of the Christian communities in a wider theological context, so too does the Apoc intend to offer a prophetic-theological interpretation of the concrete situations and problems of its communities.

This attempt to combine exhortation and theological interpretation is a characteristic which the Apoc shares not only with the Pauline literature but also with other early Christian apocalyptic writings. Such literary witnesses of early Christian apocalyptic thought are the Synoptic Gospel source Q (represented in the texts common to Luke and Matthew) and the apocalyptic discourse, Mk 13.

An intense eschatological expectation characterizes the theology of the Sayings-source Q and the community standing behind it. By interpreting their own time in the light of the imminent parousia of the Son of Man and the arrival of the kingdom of God (Lk 10:9; 22:30), the members of the Q community express their future expectations in apocalyptic-eschatological terms. They not only expect the return of Jesus as the Son of Man in the very near future, but they also judge their own time, the time before the end, to be of crucial importance (Lk 12:40). If the last judgment is at hand, it is necessary to know how to live in order to escape condemnation (Lk 17:28). Like the author of the Apoc the Logia-source

Q views the last time as a time of faithful discipleship and suffering (Lk 12:8-9). Since the members of the Q community understand themselves as prophets, they expect to share in the fate of the OT prophets (Lk 6:22-23). Just as the earlier prophets and Jesus himself were persecuted and executed (Lk 11:47-51; 13:34), so too will the true disciples of the prophet Jesus have to endure persecution and suffer death. Like the Apoc, Q combines eschatological imminent expectation with the prophetic exhortation to be faithful until death.

In ch. 13 Mark draws on an apocalyptic source or midrash (13:7-8, 14-20, 24-27). Whereas this source originally exhibited an apocalyptic mindset and speculation, Mark uses the apocalyptic material to prophetically interpret the situation of his community in the endtime. This community evidently experiences the delay of the parousia and suffers persecutions and violence because of its faith-confession in Jesus Christ (13:9-13). In such a situation Mark insists that no apocalyptic time-table is available to the Christians (13:5-6, 21-23). Only God knows when the last events are to come (13:32). The believers' task is to bear testimony to Jesus (13:9-10) and to remain faithful to the Gospel in the present period of persecution (13:12-13). They must wait diligently for the arrival of their Lord who will come when least expected (13:33-37).

Mark's editorial activity thus shows his interest in prophetic exhortation and theological interpretation rather than in apocalyptic preoccupation

23

with the establishment of a time-table for the final eschatological events. This can be seen in Mark's redactional modifications of his source. First, by adding the clauses "but the end is not yet" (13:7), "this is but the beginning of the sufferings" (13:8), and "the gospel must first be preached to all nations" (13:10), Mark interrupts and slows down the unfolding of the apocalyptic process. Secondly, the redactional additions of verses 5-6, 9-13, 21-23, 28-37 to the apocalyptic material of his source serve to interpret the significance of the time before the end for the believer. Mark begins and ends the apocalyptic discourse with the prophetic exhortation to "take heed" (13:5-6) and "to watch" (13:28-37). Moreover, he focuses the apocalyptic material by adding a reference to the situation and task of the Christian community in the time before the end (13:9-13). Finally, he destroys the sense of apocalyptic immediacy underlying 13:19-20, 24-27 by inserting verses 21-23 into their present context. In Mark the apocalyptic vision serves thus to interpret the sufferings of the community and to reinforce its witness for the gospel.

In sum, an analysis of the Logia-source Q and the apocalyptic discourse of Mk 13 shows that one of the peculiarities of early Christian apocalypticism is a combination of apocalyptic vision and exhortation for the sake of prophetic interpretation. Whereas in Judaism apocalypticism is the successor of prophecy, the early Christians claim that prophecy is again bestowed unto them as the gift of the endtime. Early Christian theology thus conceives of prophecy in apocalyptic terms. Apocalyptic imagery and vision become the vehicle for expressing prophetic interpretation and exhortation.

Like the other early Christian apocalyptic writings, the Apoc employs apocalyptic language and vision for the sake of prophetic interpretation. Apocalyptic vision and imagery serve prophetic admonition. Therefore, the author begins and ends his book with admonitions in the form of vision. Moreover, the central chapters of the Apoc (10-14) are explicitly characterized as prophetic interpretation of the political-religious situation of the Christians in the short time before the end.

Finally, the basic movement of thought and action in the Apoc is the prophetic movement from promise to fulfillment. The eschatological promises at the end of the so-called seven letters in the beginning of the book are described as fulfilled in the visions of the New Jerusalem at the end of the book. This linear-prophetic movement from promise to fulfillment appears to be deflected by the cyclic form of the three plague septetts. Yet these septetts are broken cycles insofar as their sequence moves to a greater and greater impact of the eschatological plagues until the wrath of God is fulfilled. However, even these apocalyptic plague-visions are interrupted by calls to repentance, by threats and blessings, by prophetic interpretation and visions of eschatological salvation. It is therefore evident that these apocalyptic visions also serve the prophetic purpose of exhortation. Theology and ethics, myth and vision are kept in creative tension. All this will become clearer in Chapters IV and V where more detailed analyses are provided.

In conclusion: The author of the Apoc wrote a prophetic work which is executed in the same manner as other early Christian apocalyptic writings. The apocalyptic language and imagery of the book serve prophetic interpretation and ethical admonition. The author has used dramatic, liturgical, apocalyptic and prophetic patterns and language to formulate his own literary account of early Christian prophecy.

Chapter III
TECHNIQUES OF COMPOSITION

We have seen that the total form or gestalt of the Apoc can best be defined as a literary created vision or apocalyptic-prophetic book set within an epistolary framework. This chapter proposes to explore how the author created this unique literary work.

a. The incorporation of traditional mythic patterns

The Apoc clearly employs the language of myth. Its mythic worldview divides the universe into heaven, earth, and underworld which are inhabited by angels and demons. The book speaks of great portents in heaven, of sacred books and of seven stars. Furthermore, its animal figures speak and act. The book contains elements of traditional mythologies, for example, the birth of the divine child, the sacred wedding, the divine polis, the divine warrior, and the battle between Michael and the primevil snake. The author employs sacred numbers which are elements of the astrological myth of late antiquity. The number seven, which was already in Jewish apocalypticism the number of divine perfection and holiness, functions as a structural element in the composition of the book. The four septetts (the messages, seals, trumpets, and bowls) decisively structure the book. (It has therefore been claimed that the whole plan and composition of the Apoc is patterned after the number seven. Some reconstruct seven series of seven, whereas others recogniz only five or six seven-series. However, it is difficult to explain why the author clearly marked four septettes, but did not mark the others since the existing seven series prove that he was quite capable of doing so.) Since the author does not employ discursive, logical patterns but speaks in the language of symbol and myth, his images are "open-ended" and cannot be nailed down to one single definite interpretation.

Moreover, it is difficult to understand the images and symbols of the Apoc because the author for the most part did not freely create his materials. Instead he employed traditional materials, especially from the OT, Jewish apocalypticism, pagan and Jewish myths, and early Christian traditions. To express his own theological vision he reworked them into a new and unique composition. The Apoc therefore appears on the one hand to be an artificial construction and on the other hand an artistic mosaic of poetical conciseness.

The author does not quote his materials verbatim nor does he copy them exactly; but rather he reworks and rephrases them, whenever necessary, in order to make his own theological-visionary statement. This method can clearly be detected in his use of OT traditions and texts. A good example of this compositional technique is the inaugural vision in Apoc 1:12-20 which follows closely the text and outline of Dn 10. Like the vision in Dn 10, the inaugural vision has two parts: a vision ("I saw") and audition ("I heard"). It is, however, interesting to note that the author alters the description of Dn 10 with features from Dn 7 (the son of man characterization and the description of the hair), from Exodus (the description of the robe and the girdle), and from Ezekiel (the characterization of the feet and the voice). Moreover, he expands the audition with an "I am" saying, derived from the early Christian tradition ("I am the first and the last, the living one who was dead; now I am alive forever . . ."). Finally the symbols of the seven lampstands and stars and their interpretation in Apoc 1:20 cannot be derived from the OT nor from early Christian literature. The author may have gleaned them from contemporary Judaism (cf. the menorah as the symbol of the Jewish people) or from astral religion or from the Emperor cult (the seven stars in the right hand).

Yet not only single visions or images are composed from various traditional elements and altered according to the author's purpose, but also whole sections follow the same technique and method. For instance, the so-called seven letters to the churches in Asia Minor, the first septett of the composition, are carefully composed as prophetic messenger speeches or manifestos. Each message follows a definite pattern, whose constant elements are: The address and command to write, the so-called messenger formula which is found in the Hebrew prophetic speech ("Thus says the Lord"), the call to hear, and the promise to the victorious. The main section of each letter, the I-Know section, contains several elements: A description of the situation ("I know that"), censure ("But I have against you"), call to repentance, revelatory saying with the introduction "see," the announcement of the Lord's coming and finally an exhortation and warning. Despite this uniformity of structure the seven messages are not monotonous. Four of them contain both praise and censure (I, III, IV, V); two communities receive only praise (II, VI) and one only censure (VII).

Other patterns found in the Apoc are the ritual pattern of the heavenly assembly (ch. 5), the pattern of the Holy War (19:11-22:5), the pattern of the exodus plagues (the three septetts of the eschatological plagues), and the mythic

29

pattern of the "woman with the eternal child" in 12:1-5.

Let us single out this last pattern for more comment. The myth of the queen of heaven with the eternal child is international. The elements of this myth are: the figure of the woman, the dragon, the child itself, his birth and his ascension. The myth is found in Babylon (Damkina, Marduk, Tiamat), Egypt (Hathor/Isis, Horus, Set/Typhon) in Greece (Leto, Apollo, Python) and in Palestine (Mother Zion/Israel, Messiah, Satan/Behemoth/Leviathan). In each of these myths the dragon seeks the child, not yet born, in order to devour or kill him. The woman still pregnant is pursued for the child she carries. She gives birth with the dragon only moments away, and the male-child she has just delivered is caught up to the Heavens, safe from the dragon's reach.

This myth was in use in John's time within the framework of the Roman emperor-cult. In application, the emperor's godliness was seen as his assumption of the role of the divine child, born of the goddess Roma, Queen of Heaven. The Jews also incorporated this myth into their messianic expectations. The story concerns Mother Zion who would bring forth the sons of the messianic times (Is 66:7-9). The birth-motif developed in Judaic thinking into an expectation of the birth of one son, the Deliver/Redeemer/Messiah.

The interpretation of John's use of the myth is grounded in a realization of pagan hopes for a hero-king and the Judaic expectation of a messiah.

Positing the woman as the Queen of Heaven, as Mother Zion, or as the elect community of believers, and the Dragon as the opposing force Devil/Satan, the child is clearly to be seen as the Redeemer. In John's theology, this child-god was the Christ Jesus. This last example best shows how the author works with associations of very different mythic traditions and appeals to the imagination of Jews and Hellenists alike.

b. *Literary Means of Integration*

Since the incorporation of traditional patterns of very different origin has the tendency to disrupt the unitary character of the narrative as a whole, the author has employed certain literary techniques to integrate the various traditional patterns and symbols into the literary movement of the work. Therefore, the Apoc is not encyclopedic, but dramatic in character.

As we have already seen, such a means of composition involves the *revision and variation* of traditional forms or patterns. Another means to achieve a unitary impression is the use of a *common stock of symbols* and images. In the Apoc each individual vision does not have its own exclusive set of symbols which are not found in the other visions of the book. The main symbols and images are distributed over the whole book (cf. the image of the throne or the symbol white). The author, moreover, underlines the unitary character of the work through image-clusters and symbol-associations (e.g., the image of the throne has to be seen in connection with other expressions and symbols of kingship in order to grasp its full impact. Or the notion of the eschatological "war" is intensified and enhanced by a variety of war-terminology and symbols of war). Further techniques of composition are *pre-announcements* (e.g., the promises to the victor (2:7, etc.) are repeated in ch. 21-22; the announcement of the final judgment in 14:6-20 is developed in ch. 17-20), *cross references* (e.g. the characterizations of Christ in the inaugural vision recur in ch. 2-3; the characterization of the figure as someone like a son of man is found in 14:14. Moreover, features of the figure in 1:12-20 recur in 19:11ff.; a more careful investigation could highlight many more such cross references), and *contrasts* (e.g., the beast is a contrast figure to the Lamb; the great harlot is a contrast image to the woman in ch. 12 as well as to the bride of the Lamb and the New Jerusalem).

A primary means chosen by the author to achieve an interwoven texture and unitary composition is the use of *numbers* and *numerical structures*. Basic numerical structural component forms are the four septetts and the two commissioning book visions. The septetts are again structured into four and three groupings. This interweaving of the visions in a numerical way has the effect of combining a cyclic form of repetition with a continuous forward movement. This forward movement characterizes the Apoc as end-oriented rather than encyclopedic. The forward thrust of the narrative is balanced through *interludes* which are visions of eschatological protection and salvation (e.g., 7:1-17; 11:14-19; 12:10; 14:1-5; 15:2-4; 19:1-8; 20: 4-6). Insofar as the author interrupts the patterns of continuous narrative and cyclic repetition through the insertion of these anticipatory visions, he expresses in his composition the relationship between the present situation and the eschatological future which already informs the present reality.

Very important for the composition are the techniques of *intercalation* and of *interlocking or interlacing* of texts which make a diagramming of the successive sections of the Apoc almost impossible. The method of *intercalation* is transformed by the author in the following way: He narrates in two episodes (A and A₁) what essentially belongs together. Between these two episodes he then intercalates another scene (B) and thus requires the reader to see the combined texts as a indivisible whole. For example: After the appearance of the seven angels with the seven trumpets in 8:2 (A) there follows a heavenly liturgy (B) and then the narrative returns in v. 6 to the seven angels (A₁). The same technique is employed in 17:1-22:9. Apoc 17:1-19:10 is A; 19:11-21:8 is B; 21:9-22:9 is A₁.

The method of *interlocking or interlacing* presents the greatest obstacle to our mind since we are trained to divide a literary work into sections (from the Latin secare) which follow each other and can be divided from each other. The author of the Apoc does not *divide* the text into separate slices or sections but *joins* them together

33

by employing the technique of interlocking or interlacing. This is done by inserting into the preceding section a passage or part which clearly belongs also to the following section. Such an example of interlacing is Apoc 10:1-11:14. This section is clearly an interlude incorporated into the trumpet septett analogous to ch. 7. At the same time the section clearly belongs, from a contentual point of view, to the following section ch. 12-14 since it refers to the beast and to the same time period as ch. 12 and 13.

In the total composition of the book the author combines the techniques of inclusion, interlacing, and the numerical seven pattern in order to weave the single visions, auditions, and admonitions together into a unique whole. Yet the same compositional techniques make it hard for the modern reader, who thinks in a linear-logical fashion, to comprehend the outline and plan of the book. Since we expect a linear temporal sequence, we are startled by the interrludes, the proleptic descriptions of eschatological salvation, and the apparent repetitions. The Apoc on the whole is not cyclic but moves forward from promise to fulfillment. Yet this movement of symbol and thought is not linear-logical or linear-temporal, but can best be envisioned as a spiral moving from the present situation of the Christian communities in Asia Minor to the eschatological salvation of the New Jerusalem. This development of thought is not chronological but topical or thematical. It can be likened to a musical theme or motif with variations, each variation enhancing and moving the total composition.

The movement of symbol and thought in the Apoc could also be likened to that of a dramatic motion picture with several acts whose individual scenes portray the action or the actors of the plot from a different angle or perspective. In order to understand more fully these compositional techniques and perspectives of the author we have to analyze more carefully the content and plan of the book as a whole.

CHAPTER IV

CONTENT AND PLAN OF THE APOCALYPSE

As a literary work the Apoc begins with a headline, which spells out the correct title of the book: Revelation (Apocalypse) of Jesus Christ to John to the seven communities in Asia Minor. In the beginning the author gives the instruction that the book should be read aloud in the assembly of the community. After the introduction there are an epistolary address (1:4-6), a prophetic announcement and a direct word of God (1:7-8) that the revelation of "what must happen soon" is warranted by God.

a. The basic outline of the Apoc

The first commissioning vision of the book (1:

35

9-20) is introduced by a statement about the author and his situation. John calls himself a brother of his readers and states that because of his Christian witness he was exiled to the Island Patmos. He states that he has received his revelations on the "day of the Lord," Sunday, but he does not mention in which year.

The old tradition according to which the Apoc was written in the last years of the Emperor Domitian, i.e., between 90-96 A.D. is widely accepted today. The commissioning or inaugural vision (1:12-20) is closely linked to the so-called seven letters (ch. 2-3), insofar as all descriptions of the Christ-figure are repeated in the beginning of the messages. A new commissioning or inaugural vision in ch. 4-5 shows the reader the throne-room of God in heaven and the endowment of the Lamb with the seven sealed scroll which is opened in the seven seal visions (ch. 6-7). The seal-septett is followed by a second seven series, the trumpets of the wrath of God (ch. 8-9; 11:14-19). Ch. 10-11 contain two further commissionings of the seer and describe the fate of the two witnesses. Ch. 12 introduces the "great portent in heaven" — the woman clad with the sun, the male child, and the dragon, whereas ch. 13 portrays the two allies of the dragon, the beast from the sea and the beast from the land which are characterized with political-religious features. Ch. 14 shows the Lamb with the 144,000 on Mount Sion (14:15) and announces the final judgment (14:6-20). The last septett of the bowls (ch. 15-16) is followed by a description of the great world city Babylon and its destruction (ch. 17-18). The victory song of the heavenly world (19:1-8) is followed by the description of the coming of Christ in judgment, the destruction of the two beasts (ch. 19), the binding and destruction of the dragon, and the thousand year messianic reign. This series of judgments is closed with the scene of the final judgment (ch. 20). The whole book reaches its climax in the visions of the new world and of the New Jerusalem (21:1-22:5). The author concludes the long series of visions and auditions with an epilogue, containing sanctions, the early Christian prayer "Come Lord Jesus," and a final greeting (22:6-21).

It would be of great help if we could rediscover *the* structuring or organizing principle which the author had in mind when writing the book. Since this is no longer possible, the following attempt to order the contents of the book remains hypothetical, but it might prove helpful. It presupposes the preceding discussions on the literary techniques employed by the author.

All exegetes agree that 1:9-3:21 form the first section of the book. It is also clear that the last section of the book, the visions of the eschatological salvation (21:1-22:5) are a unit of their own. Most exegetes would begin this unit with the parousia vision of 19:11-16. The main part of the book, 4:1—19:10, is divided into two sections by the two "scroll" commissioning visions. Ch. 4-5 are generally recognized as introducing a new vision series. The question is how far this

37

series extends. Since the seal visions (6:1—8:1) are clearly linked with the inaugural vision of ch. 4-5 on the one hand and with the septetts of the trumpets (8:2—9:21; 11:15-19) and bowls (15:1-5—16:21) which are formally and contentually a development of the seal-septett, on the other hand, we can assume that these visions belong together in the mind of the author. Apoc 4:1-9:21; 11:15-19 and 15:1,5-19:10 seem to form a literary unit, which encloses the "prophetic scroll" with Apoc 10:1-15:4. Thus we can divide the Apoc in four major contentual units:

I. 1:9-3:22: The Seven Messages to the Churches
II. 4:1-9:21; 11:15-19; 15:1,5-19:10: The Sevenfold Sealed Scroll
III. 10:1-15:4: The Prophetic Scroll
IV. 19:11-22:5: Judgment and Salvation.

This outline can only be understood when we keep in mind the author's technique of interlacing or interlocking. The first unit of the "seven letters" is connected with the last unit of the New Jerusalem, insofar as the christological features and eschatological promises of the first section are repeated in the last. Further, the prophetic scroll is on the one end interlocked with the seven sealed scroll through the interlude 10:1-11:1 and on the other end through 15:2-4 which are the climax of this unit and at the same time an interlude of the seven bowl septett. Finally the last section of the New Jerusalem is interlaced with the seven sealed scroll through ch. 17-18

38

which are on the one hand an appendix of the last bowl-plague and on the other hand form the first part of the inclusion 17:1-22:5. This last unit is also connected with the prophetic scroll insofar as 19:11-22:5 describes as fulfilled what was announced in 14:6-15.

b. Plan and Content of the Apoc

A summary interpretation of the four contentual units of the Apoc can highlight their major themes and interests.

1. The _so-called seven letters_ to the churches in Asia Minor are not real letters, but formalized proclamations of the risen Christ to the churches. They give a realistic but stylized description of the situation of the communities. The author does not idealize them but points out their strengths and weaknesses. His main objective is exhortation and critical evaluation. The strong points of the churches are: mutual love and service for others, fidelity and patient endurance, keeping the word of the Lord and rejection of the false teachings. On the whole the author places strong emphasis on the works or praxis of the communities.

However, not all churches are still doing "the works of their first love." Some of them are no longer "alive," others do not reject the message of the rival teachers, others are even in danger of being "cast away." The main exhortation therefore is the call to remember what the Lord has done for them, to repent and to endure, to hold fast to what they have. The churches of Asia Minor are threatened by Jewish persecutions, Christian rival teachers, and the Roman civil religion. The power behind this threefold opposition is Satan (cf. 2:10,12,24). All the messages close with an eschatological promise for those who remained victorious.

2. The eschatological promises and characterizations of Jesus Christ found in the first unit are all taken up again in the *final section Apoc 19:11-22:5*. The first and the final unit thus stand in close contentual relationship with each other. They frame and circle with admonitions and promises the two central sections of the Apoc. In both units exhortation and vision are interrelated insofar as the seven messages are part of the Inaugural Vision and the section on the New Jerusalem contains admonitions and promises. The concluding section ends with the blessing of Moses which is followed by the promise: "They shall reign for ever and ever" (22:3-5). This promise recalls the last promise of the seven message section: "He who conquers, I will grant him to sit with me on my throne, as I myself conquered and sat down with my Father on his throne" (3:21).

The composition of the Apoc thus builds a bridge from the present time of the Christian communities to the salvation of the eschatological future announced in the letters' promises for the victorious. The first unit looks at the churches standing under the scrutiny and protection of the risen Lord. In 19:11-22:5 the seer describes the liberation of the world from all evil powers and the salvation of the New Jerusalem, the universal community on the New Earth.

3. Chapter 5, which has as its climax the handing over of the sealed, eschatological scroll to the Lamb, forms with chapter 4 the beginning of the *central apocalyptic section of the Apoc (4:1-19:10)*. The object of the introductory vision is the choice of someone worthy to receive and open the scroll which lies in the hands of God who is characterized as the one "who sits on the throne." The contents of the scroll are clearly the eschatological catastrophes which are portrayed in the three septetts and set in motion by the opening of the seals. By taking possession of the scroll, the Lamb is enthroned as the eschatological regent of the world who is to execute the plagues of the final time on the world. In the three plague-septetts the eschatological rule of Christ over the whole world is exercised. Whereas the visions of the seals show the traditional characteristics of the endtime (Antichrist, war, hunger and death; cf. Mk 13), the septetts of the trumpets and bowls picture Yahweh's day of wrath in cosmic catastrophes as the new Exodus of the people of God from the oppression of the antidivine powers. The sequence of the plagues is not temporal-chronological but thematic-schematical. All three septetts refer to the same events. Whereas the trumpet-plagues strike only a third of the cosmos and of humanity, the bowls of wrath destroy the whole world.

4. The contents of the *"small scroll" (10:1-15:4)* which has been inserted between the

41

visions of the trumpets and those of the bowls, is explicitly characterized in ch. 10 as a "prophetic word." The two commissioning visions in 10:1-11:2 direct our attention from the cosmic heavenly events to those on earth. The seer is told to prophecy "about many peoples and nations and tongues" and to "measure" the temple and worshippers of God. The essential content of the "small scroll" is sketched in the vision of the two witnesses and unfolded in ch. 12-14. While the septetts of the plagues are of cosmic nature, the main goal of the "small scroll" is the prophetic interpretation of the situation of the persecuted Christians. The author characterizes the present situation of the community by means of the danielic phrase "a time, and times, and half a time" as the eschatological time of tribulation and of probation for the Christian community.

This time is at the same time the time of Satan and his allies, who stand behind the Roman persecution of the Christians. Satan's activity is made manifest in the actions of the beast and the false prophet. The description of the beast from the abyss is influenced not only by the danielic beasts, but also by the notion of the Antichrist. The beast is the caricature of the Lamb (13:3, 12, 14). As such it is characterized with royal features and as if slaughtered. Its main goal is to seduce people to adore the dragon (13:4). For this purpose it employs the beast from the land, the false prophet, who works miracles to seduce the dwellers of the earth into worshipping the beast and its image. The second beast persecutes and financially boycotts all those who do not accept the mark of the first beast. The satanic powers personified in the political and religious leaders of the Roman Empire dominate the whole earth. Therefore the Christians are called to resist them and to choose captivity and death rather than the idolatrous worship of the Roman civil religion. Therefore the unit Apoc 10:1-15:4 climaxes in the eschatological victory-song of those "who have conquered the beast and its image and the number of its name" (15:2).

By making the "small scroll" the formal center of his composition, the author highlights the central theme and objective of the book as a whole. The Apoc is intended to be prophetic interpretation of the situation of the Christians in Asia Minor at the end of the first century. The Apoc therefore begins with a section of censure and admonition to remain faithful. Then the major part of the book describes in mythological language the threat of the religious and political powers of Asia Minor against the Christians and points out that God and Christ are the true eschatological rulers of the world. Therefore all the earthdwellers are called to repentance, and the Christians are exhorted to faithful endurance. Finally, the last section of the Apoc shows the readers the glory of the eschatological world and salvation when all the anti-divine (the dragon, the two beasts and Babylon) and all dehumanizing powers (sorrow, persecution, death) will be destroyed.

The composition and plan of the Apoc reflects the same themes as Martin Luther King's "Letter from a Birmingham Jail." In the crude outline of this letter scribbled on toiletpaper in jail the following three topics emerge: 1) the ethics of Christian commitment; 2) the judgment of God upon the dehumanizing power, White America; and 3) a glimpse of the New Jerusalem. In the Apoc the divine judgment on the dehumanizing power, Rome, and its idolatry is followed by the vision of the new earth and the New Jerusalem. However, since exegetes frequently separate the first part of the book, the so-called seven messages, from the main so-called apocalyptic part (ch. 4-22), they often overlook the fact that the author avoids an absolute dualism by giving great prominence to ethical admonition. This ethical interest of the author prevents the reader of his time and us from projecting "evil" only onto "others" while not holding ourselves accountable. The Apoc speaks not only of vengeance against the dehumanizing and anti-divine powers, but also calls Christians as well as the inhabitants of the earth to repentance. The author insists that the Christians in no way have "made it" but are still in danger of losing their share in the New Jerusalem. The Apoc could easily give the impression that evil exists only outside the Christian community but not within it if the author had not taken care to begin the book with the great vision of the judgment of Christ on the Christian churches and to interject throughout the book eschatological warnings, ethical demands, and encouraging promises.

CHAPTER V
THE THEOLOGICAL PERSPECTIVE OF
THE APOCALYPSE

As the "jailhouse-experience" has left its marks
on the writings of Martin Luther King, Dietrich
Bonhöffer, Angela Davis or Daniel Berrigan, so
it has also deeply influenced the theological perspective of the Apoc. To overlook the fact that the
theology of the Apoc is formulated in the face
of persecution, banishment, jail and execution
would be to misunderstand the intentions and
concerns of its author.

Such "jail-house-experience" was nothing new
in early Christianity, and it left its imprints on
most of the NT writings. As Jesus was executed
as a political criminal because of his message and
ministry, so the Christians have to expect suffering and persecutions as an inescapable consequence of their faith in Jesus Christ. In 2 Cor 11:
23ff. Paul recounts the ordeals which he has
suffered because of the Gospel of Jesus Christ:
imprisonments, beatings, lashes, stonings, toils
and hardships, dangers from his own people, the
Jews, from gentiles, and from false brethren.
These persecutions led, as we know, to his final
captivity and execution.

a. The theological problem

The author of the Apoc is a political exile
because of his witness to Jesus. He knows that

the communities of Asia Minor have already suffered persecutions from the Jews as well as from the Roman authorities. He warns these communities that they have to expect even greater trials, persecutions and imprisonments. The author attempts to encourage the congregations in their difficult situation and to point out the theological meaning of their suffering and trials. He warns them not to avoid prison and death and not to fall prey to apostasy. However, whereas other NT writings as e.g., Paul, Mark or 1 Peter point to the example of the suffering and death of Jesus Christ, the author of the Apoc points to the exalted Christ, whose title is "King of Kings and Lord of Lords" (19:16). He knows that the Lamb was "slaughtered," but this knowledge of the crucified Jesus Christ does not form the center of his theology as it did for Paul.

The central theological image of Apoc is the image of the throne. Its major theological theme is the conflict between the kingdom and reign of God, Jesus Christ and the Christians, on the one hand, and that of the Beast and Babylon on the other hand. God is characterized as the Great-King "sitting on the throne" in royal splendor and power surrounded by 24 vassal kings and the heavenly court (ch. 4) who proclaim day and night: "Holy, holy, is the Lord God Almighty" (4:8). Jesus Christ shares in the throne and kingly reign of his Father because he was victorious (3:21). He is the slain Lamb (the central christological image in the Apoc). As such he alone in the whole universe is worthy to take over the seven sealed scroll and with it eschatological dominion over the world. His cosmic heavenly kingship is based on the fact that in his death he has ransomed the Christians from "every tribe, and tongue, and nation" and has made them "a kingdom and priests to our God" (5:9-10). The Christians are now the representatives of God's kingdom on earth, and they will share actively in the exercise of the divine kingship in the eschatological future (5:10; 20:6; 22:5). The affirmation that the Christians by virtue of their baptism and redemption already now share in the kingdom and kingship of Christ appears to have been one of the major theological convictions in the early Christian communities.

This faith-conviction of the early Christians in Asia Minor ran counter to their concrete everyday experience of harassment and persecution. Theology and reality contradicted each other. The Christians experienced again and again that their life and situation in no way reflected their theology of kingship, power, and glory. This tension between faith-conviction and reality-experience provoked difficult theological problems and questions: If Jesus Christ is the true Lord and King of the world, why do his followers have to suffer? If Christians share in the kingdom and royal power of God, why are they persecuted and why do they suffer deadly conflicts? If God is really in power and if Christ is the eschatological regent of the world, why do they not revenge the blood of so many Christians who have already had to die? Why did Christ not come in glory to prevent the further suffering and slaughter of the people of God? These pressing theological queries appear to have received different theological answers from leading Christian prophets in the Churches of Asia Minor. We know this from the author of the Apoc who argues against a rival Christian proposal and prophetic movement. Since we only have his words, we have to reconstruct this oppositional theological view from the accusations which the author levels against this rival theology.

b. The theological option of the opponents

The author explicitly names the opponents in his messages to the churches in Ephesus (2:1-7), Pergamum (2:12-17), and Thyatira (2:18-29). He praises the church of Ephesus for rejecting the itinerant apostles of the Nicolaitans, reproaches the church of Pergamum for tolerating them, and censures the community of Thyatira for accepting the teaching of one of their prophets whom he labels "Jezebel." As the characterization of their teaching indicates, the Nicolaitans were probably a Christian libertine group who advocated adaptation to their pagan society insofar as they ate food sacrificed to idols and advocated either sexual license or more probably religious syncretism. Since the author likens their teaching to that of Balaam and calls one of their leading prophets "Jezebel," the accusation that they committed fornication has probably to be understood in a metaphorical sense as practicing idolatry or syncretism.

The Nicolaitans' advocacy of syncretism and

adaptation to the rites of their pagan society was not only politically but also economically and professionally of great importance, since meat sacrificed to idols was served at the meetings of the trade guilds and business associations. Moreover, the money which they daily used bore the image of the divine emperor. The theological option proposed by the Nicolaitans thus allowed the Christian citizens to take part actively in the social, commercial, and political life of their society.

What were the theological reasons which allowed the Nicolaitans to opt for the syncretistic adaptation to their pagan society? What exactly was the theological issue at stake? The Nicolaitans probably argued, as the enthusiasts in Corinth had done some forty years earlier, that "idols are nothing" and that therefore the Christians could eat of the sacrifical food. Moreover, since every educated Roman knew that Caesar's claim to divinity was nothing more than a constitutional fiction to promote political loyalty to the Roman state, why should the Christians refuse to pay the honor and loyalty due the Emperor? Did not the great Apostle Paul demand that one submit to the authorities of the state because they were ordained by God (Rm 13:1-7)? Since loyalty to the Roman civil religion does not necessarily involve creedal statements but only participation in certain cultic ceremonies, it is possible to participate in the emperor cult without denying one's faith in Jesus Christ.

If participation in the ceremonies and rituals

of the Roman civil religion is only an expression of one's political loyalty but not of one's religious faith, it would be foolish to make it a theological issue. To oppose the emperor cult and to risk one's life for this opposition would mean taking the kingship claims of the Roman emperor and state too seriously. The Christians confess that not the Roman emperor but Jesus Christ is the true Lord of the universe and the human soul. The Christians are taken out of this world, and by virtue of their baptism they already share in the kingly power and priestly dignity of their Lord (1:6). No one, not even Satan, can harm the elect Christians, since they have insight into the very depths of the demonic and since they share in the spiritual community of the divine, heavenly world. If this is the case, they why go to prison or to death for a cause which is theologically not worth dying for? Did not the Apostle Paul agree that idols have no real existence (1 Cor 8:4)? Moreover, Christians are certain that the image of Caesar is nothing more than an idol, aren't they? To say otherwise would be bad theology or religious fanaticism.

The author of the Apoc had to respond to this theological challenge in such a way that he maintained the early Christian faith-confession and at the same time convincingly showed how dangerous the theology of the Nicolaitans was.

c. The theological perspective of the author

The author of the Apoc puts forth an alternative theological interpretation to the Christian communities of Asia Minor. Both his sharp rejection of the Nicolaitans in the so-called seven letters and his urgent denunciation of the imperial cult in the main part of the book are interdependent. The so-called letters and the apocalyptic visions of the Apoc address the same situation and theological problem.

John affirms that Jesus Christ is the Lord and King of the world. He also repeats the early Christian baptismal confession that Christ made the baptized a kingdom and appointed them priests (1:6). However, he does not understand the kingdom of God and Christ in an individualistic-spiritualizing way but conceives of it in political-universal terms. Rome and the Roman Caesar have real power on earth. They are not "nothing." Behind their kingship and kingdom is Satan, the anti-divine power par excellence. To acknowledge the emperor and his cult means to deny Christ's claim to Lordship and reign over the world and nations. If Christians belong to the kingdom of God, they cannot at the same time be loyal citizens of the Roman emperor and state which claim the divine power and honors due to God and Christ. Loyalty to the Roman empire implies treason and betrayal of the kingdom and power of God. This either-or situation is forced upon the Christians by the absolute claim of dominion and divine power by the Roman ruling power. Those rejecting the beast and its cult are excluded from economic and social life on earth (13:16) and have to accept captivity and death (13:10). The Apoc demands unfaltering resistance to the imperial cult because to give divine honors to the emperor would mean to ratify his claim of power and dominion over all people and nations. Thus the power struggle between the two kingdoms is absolute; no neutral stance is possible.

A co-existence between the kingdom of God and the kingdom of Rome is not possible for the author of the Apoc. Like Jewish eschatology he understands the royal expressions, "kingdom, kingship, reign" not in a spiritualistic sense as pertaining only to the individual soul or to the heavenly realm, but he conceives of them as concrete political-societal realities. As the exalted Lord, Christ has assumed kingship and power over the world and all nations. He rules now in heaven. The Christians are the deputies of his kingdom and reign on earth. Therefore they are, by virtue of their redemption, the universal anti-empire to the Roman empire which has also universalistic claims. Eschatological salvation means the abolishment of the Roman empire and its idolatrous-dehumanizing forces. The establishment of the kingdom of God and the dominion of Christ on a new earth will replace them in the eschatological future. In the New Jerusalem God's throne will be among God's people and the loyal Christians will rule with Christ forever and ever. In the meanwhile, however, the Christians are still in danger of losing their share in the kingship of God by giving the emperor honors which belong to God and Christ as the true rulers of the nations. The author can advocate such a sharp rejection of the Roman empire because he is convinced that the power of God and Christ will prevail over the anti-divine forces. A victory of God, Christ and the loyal Christians is at hand, and God's kingship will very soon be exercised on earth as it is now in heaven.

The author describes in three steps how the dominion of Christ and God takes hold of the world and universe. God's rule is now the reality of heaven. In the eschatological plagues and in the parousia of Christ it extends to the earth. Finally it will destroy all antidivine powers, Death and Underworld. In his exaltation Christ, the Lamb, has received the eschatological rule and kingship in heaven. The Lamb was worthy to receive glory and power because he has created a kingly community of those redeemed from all peoples, tongues and nations (ch. 5). At the same time Satan is thrown down to earth, where he rules through the Roman emperor and state for a short while (ch. 12-13). The representatives of the dominion of Christ and of Satan are therefore pitted against each other in the short time before the end. With the parousia of Christ the second step is taken (19:11-20:6): Christ and the faithful Christians assume kingship over the world on earth. Babylon-Rome is destroyed, the two beasts are imprisoned, and Satan is thrown into the abyss. Finally, Satan, Death and Hades are destroyed; all persons are judged according to their works (20:7-15), and a new heaven and new earth appear (21:1-22:5). The New Jerusalem comes down from heaven and God thrones among God's people. Then those who have rejected the worship of the beast and its image serve God as priests and exercise their kingship for ever and ever. The center of the theological movement of the Apoc is the earth, as the following diagram indicates.

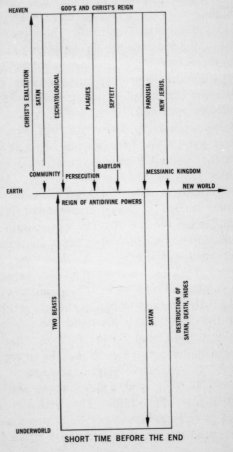

The central theological question of the Apoc is:
To whom does the earth belong? Who is the ruler
of this world? The Christian claim that Jesus
Christ is not a mere cultic god but the Lord of the
world necessarily had to come in conflict with
the proclamation of the Roman civil religion:
Caesar is Lord and God. Thus the Christian confession "Jesus Christ is the Lord of the earth"
was a profoundly political assertion. This assertion has as its consequence the understanding of
Christian existence in political-religious terms:
The Christians are the deputies of the divine
Lordship on earth. They are witnesses to God's
and Christ's claim of the earth. Their goal is not
to subdue the world but to defend their Lord's
claim to the earth. They do not now have the
political power to overthrow the illegitimate rulers
of the earth, but they maintain that the one who
"makes all things new" and the one who is the
"Lord of Lords and King of Kings" are coming
soon and will not delay. God's and Christ's coming and reign mean salvation not only for the
Christians but also for all those now slaughtered
and suffering on earth. At the same time God's
and Christ's judgment and reign entail the destruction of all those who "corrupt the earth."

The power behind the political domination
which "corrupts the earth" is Satan, the anti-divine power par excellence. Whereas the heavens
rejoice over the devil's downfall, the world is in
anguish:

"Woe to you, o earth and sea

for the devil has come down to you in great
wrath
because he knows that his time is short"
(12:12).

The dragon-devil gave the beast from the sea,
the Roman emperor, "his power and his throne
and his great authority" (13:2). This power of
the Roman empire appears to be absolute and
universal. It affects Christians and non-Christians
alike:

> "Also it was allowed to make war on the saints
> and to conquer them. And authority was given
> it over every tribe and people and tongue and
> nation, and all who dwell on earth will worship
> it . . ." (13:7f.).

As God's deputies on earth (1:6; 5:10) the
Christians are by definition the enemies of the
totalitarian Roman world-empire and of its allies.
The dwellers of the earth, the free and the slaves,
the merchants and kings of the earth submit to the
power of this empire which corrupts and devas-
tates the earth. Therefore the outcries of the
Christians for justice and judgment (6:9; 15:4;
18:20) are also on behalf of the earth (20:4-6).
God's justice and human salvation coincide (21:
1-7). God's coming in judgment means justice for
those who rejected the oppression of the great
world power Babylon-Rome which "corrupts the
earth" (19:2). It brings judgment on those who
usurped God's and Christ's lordship over the
earth. Both aspects of God's coming and judgment
are expressed in the eschatological victory-hymn:

56

"We give thanks to thee, Lord, God, Almighty
who art and wast
that thou hast taken thy great power
and begun to reign.
The nations raged, but thy wrath came,
and the time for the dead to be judged
for rewarding thy servants, the prophets and
    saints
and those who fear thy name, both small and
    great
and for destroying the destroyers of the earth"
    (11:17f.).

God's judgment and reign which is here announced in hymnic praise, is described in the final
visions of the Apoc. Babylon, the two beasts, and
finally the dragon are overcome and punished.
The last enemies to be judged are the powers
Death and Hades. The new earth is a earth without any destructive and oppressive powers. God's
judgment means salvation for the earth and all
humankind.

This new earth and world therefore will be
completely different from the earth and world of
suffering and death which we know and experience. God's reign cannot coexist with any dehumanizing power which destroys the earth. The
first heaven and the first earth, the dualism between God's and Christ's dominion and those
of the devil and Rome will give room to a new
heaven and a new earth. The author of the Apoc
does not envision, as Paul did, that at the Last
Day the Christians "shall be caught up together
with them [the dead] in the clouds to meet the
Lord" (1 Thes 4:17), but sees the New Jerusalem,

the holy city of humankind, "coming down out of heaven from God" (21:2). The voice from the throne pronounces final salvation on a new earth:

"Behold the dwelling of God is with human beings.
He will dwell with them, and they shall be his people
And God himself will be with them;
He will wipe every tear from their eyes,
and death shall be no more,
neither shall there be mourning nor crying nor pain any more
for the former things have passed away"
(21:3-4).

Whereas the dominion of Rome was characterized by darkness, blood and death, the new city of humankind under the dominion of God is full of light, richness, and life. As Rome had the kings of the earth and all the nations as its subjects, so in the glory and splendor of the New Jerusalem

". . . shall the nations walk,
and the kings of the earth shall bring their glory into it . . .
they shall bring into it the glory and honor of the nations" (21:24, 26).

The faithful Christians, however, who risked their life in rejecting the idolatrous Roman power, will exercise their kingly power with Jesus Christ in the new world (5:10; 20:4-6; 22:5). In the eschatological future the faithful deputies of God's and Christ's reign on earth will actively participate in the divine reign and power.

In the face of persecution and oppression by the political powers of the time the author asserts that the Christians are appointed to kingship, and that they are members of God's kingdom on earth. However, he also maintains that it would be an illusion if the Christians would think that they already now share in the active exercise of God's and Christ's kingly power. As Jesus Christ's exaltation and installation as ruler of the world had as its precondition his victory in death, so the Christian's exercise of kingly power in the eschatological future is based upon their conquering of persecution and death. By remaining steadfast in persecution and death, they like Christ gain the right to rule in the New Jerusalem. Therefore, the author of the Apoc cannot assign to the Christians an active part in the overthrow of the political and demonic powers "who destroy the earth" in the short time before the end. He, however, also cannot envision eternal life and salvation without the creation of a new earth. Whereas the Fourth Gospel can proclaim that the believers have gained final salvation and eternal life in their acceptance of Jesus in faith, the author of the Apoc cannot envision a spiritualized presentic salvation but maintains that eternal life and salvation have to include the earth and full humanity.

CONCLUSION

This concrete-political understanding of eschatological salvation as the non-oppressive kingdom and dominion of God and Jesus Christ has not so much influenced mainline Christianity as it has inspired Christian chiliastic movements. Whereas established Christianity has more and more conceived of salvation as the spiritual salvation of the soul, the messianic movements within Christianity have again and again affirmed the Apoc's vision of salvation as an earthly, political reality, as liberation from the oppressive conditions of domination in this world. They have maintained that salvation means the establishment of the reign of God in this world and not merely the salvation of the soul from this world.

Whereas established Christianity has accepted the opponent's theological option of adaptation to the present societal ruling powers because they cannot touch the salvation of the soul, the messianic movements within Christianity have always maintained that oppressive political powers and Christian salvation cannot coexist. Even though they often assumed a greater active participation of the Christians in the establishment of God's kingdom on earth than the author of the Apoc did, they nevertheless hoped for eschatological salvation on a "New Earth," freed from all oppressive and dehumanizing powers. The attempt by the author of the Apoc to formulate the reality and meaning of eschatological salvation not only in spiritual-religious, but also in universal-political terms gains greater significance today in the face of theological attempts to formulate a political theology or a theology of liberation.

REVIEW and STUDY QUESTIONS

1. Why are you interested in the Apocalypse?
2. Which interpretations of the Apocalypse do you know?
3. Describe the literary models which the author used.
4. Why can the Apocalypse be defined as a "prophetic-apocalyptic circular letter"?
5. How did the author use his traditions and materials?
6. Explain some of the compositional techniques of the author. Why is it important to know them?
7. Describe the major sections of the Apocalypse.
8. Why is it important to note that the author criticises and admonishes the Christian churches?
9. Which theological situation and problem does the Apocalypse address?

10. Who are the Nicolaitans? Describe their theological proposal. pp48, 49

11. Develop the theological perspective of the author: What is his notion of kingship and power? Why do Christians have to reject the Roman civil religion? How does the author envision the eschatological future?

12. Does the Apocalypse have any theological relevance for today?